This Country of Gale-force Winds

This Country of Gale-force Winds

Eileen Hennessy

NYQ Books™

The New York Quarterly Foundation, Inc.
New York, New York

NYQ Books™ is an imprint of The New York Quarterly Foundation, Inc.

The New York Quarterly Foundation, Inc.
P. O. Box 2015
Old Chelsea Station
New York, NY 10113

www.nyqbooks.org

First Edition

Set in New Baskerville

Layout and Design by Raymond P. Hammond

Cover Design by Caroline Evans

Cover Illustration: "The Hurricane"
© Mariagrazia Orlandini | Dreamstime.com

Library of Congress Control Number: 2011940335

ISBN: 978-1-935520-52-8

This Country of Gale-force Winds

Contents

I.

II.

III.

To all our ancestors, with profound thanks.

I.

Eight things a day, that's all

they ask us to declare.
We know you have billions, they say.
So we take our places in the line
and say what words we can.
On the quiet side, there's
declaring to Customs,
declaring to a court,
declaring income for taxes.
There are also declarations
of intent and love and truth-telling,

but here
we're moving toward the wilder side,
a chilly wind blows, a white
plastic bag chatters along a path,
angels of the Lord declare,
Here's where you'll build your town.
So we take our places in the line
and pile word on word into houses,
build the stories we live by.
Out here. On this sandy coast.
In this country of gale-force winds.

Landscape with freight train

The simplicity of your string of boxcars
banging into a village.
Oil stains on the ties,
moss and weeds between the cinders,
metal striking metal. The church bells
clang to a halt. Doors close
behind the last of the faithful
to arrive, anxious and puffing,
for ten o'clock Mass. The village cats
shuffle to the river. Sunday love
between a cat and a fish
is a rare and precious thing.

The simplicity of the chaplet of villages
strung on the single track. Your train
makes its rounds, arrives back
at the junction, is shunted to the siding.
Don't assume that your mere presence there
makes you superior. Get out,
tap a tree, collect the sap on a rag,
look for wounds to bind.

Sometimes he thinks about walking

on another side of the world.
Once, when he was seven,
a Governor patted him on the head,
asked how he was going to move
through the open-wide spaces
of the state. He was not
going anywhere then, he stood
at every water-green light,
gawked at the trucks hauling
Christmas trees, women
balancing gifts in their arms.

He walks to work, an hour away,
door to door. The road is paved
with tiny rattling thoughts
that fly up, nick his face. Sometimes
he thinks he'll never get there.
Believes not everything
should be in people's front yards,
but there shouldn't be nothing in them,
otherwise he's not safe
walking door to door, yard to yard,
looking for a footing.

Cold comfort

The lobsters climb to my shoulders,
days when the weather's warm.
Drink my cocktail, look out
at the world up front. Sweet creatures.
They've been known to climb
to the dairy farm on the roof-garden
where there's time for turned milk,
warm butter to spread on our bread,
a place for my kids to play ball,
kick the cow patties. Days of worship,
I take the kids to the aquarium temple
to fish for dinner, mostly
catfish, starfish, jellyfish,
none of the great wild fish
that would decorate my table
if it were big enough for free-range dining.
There are days that are made for talking,
days that are made for doing. My timing's
always off, what with mercury-mind
dipping low, sliding into the food-chain.
At least there's sunlight on my raisins.
At least I know how to eat green.
Little things that make me famous.

Yet another bout of meaningful madness

Where I live now, the hot ticket is
little box houses
heated by a bed of coals
in the living-room fireplace.
It's cheap coal, and there isn't
much of it. I'm in the background,

not broadcasting, just receiving.
When last we talked, I had just left
a weathervane rooster sniveling
above a small yard with a small
wooden house where I could kick up,
put my feet back, close my eyes

to the world pressing on the windows.
I was solid, sturdy, dependable,
beautifully simple. That gone-by self
is still so bright. I've figured out

what causes the glitch in my landscape:
The cabbage roses staring
out of the wallpaper. The part of me
that wants to shine wildly,
an angel in a tarnished pewter sky.

That most American thing

Think hand upon haft,
hand gripping shield,
hand swatting flies
from the faces of the dead,
hand on the rudder of the boat.

Think glad hand that grasps.

If your right hand offends you,
cut it off. Your neighbor
will exchange the handshake of peace
with someone else.

And if your left hand offends you?

Those of us who remember

the second great last just war
remember when the bravest of waters
were British: Firth of Forth,
Firth of Clyde, Tyne, Mersey.

Irish-American Catholic child,
I had only the Atlantic, peaceful
where it pushed against my shores. I
lived among ancestral ghosts:

hewers of wood and drawers of water
who had fled the Shannon, Liffey, Lee,
Boyne, Galway Bay—haunted routes
of escape to any-other-place far enough

from Protestant British Occupation. To us
who remember the America where
everything finest and best was British,
other things seem possible now:

parting the sea, walking on the waves,
even casting a net and pulling in
multitudes of fish that can swim
side by side, not touching, at ease.

Poem for Memorial Day

1.

Nowadays we need
more than one string on the old violin,
even if we're careful to draw the bow
across a different spot each time.
Even then: The string makes a sound
between sob and sigh, tentative plaint,
not the *thwang!* of an arrow
leaping from the cord

in the Saturday afternoon movie house
with arrows flying, cowboys and Indians,
cavalry bullets clearing the road
to the West, we kids cheering
pioneer grit, hands fast with a gun,
finger on trigger, dirt under the nails
that won the world and lost

America. Welcome to the parched riverrun
where our squirrels come to die.
This is banjo land, guitar at best,
twang, twang. X marks the states
where we fell, one place at a time,
one day at a time. No reason
not to stroke a back,
rub oil on its raw spots.
We're in for a long straight spell of drought.

2.

Throngs of blowfish-shaped women. Tufts of feathery hair,
round-bellied men who park their trucks around the main
square, and a big-haired ginger cat that attends to tittering
birds. Blooms of sunshine tumble through the treetops. The
sunlight has been here for years. Under the close-fitting sky,
thoughts flit among the houses. Fat mice jump from step to
step down front stoops. The cat goes into crouch and creep,
springs. Crunch of bird-bones fine as feather shafts. The
children not heard, not seen.

United States Poem

Metal was the thing, the only thing.
Metal of madness, metal of change
for the bus, our pocket seams reamed

by coins. Every screaming buffalo
nickel was squeezed. We still had
the beach house, we sat and waited

for the tide to haul in the iron
age of profit. We were promised

a dime roll on the White House lawn,
circlets of silver wheeling,
our change in gold,

everything good that could come to us
from Serving with Honor
For Cat and House, For Mat and Mouse,

or some such phrase apt

(for God and Country, *that's* what it was)

for the crashing of church bells,
the drumrolled dirge
for our honored dead. Once that
was over and done with, they sent us

peanut butter and jelly,
American cheese with pickle supine
on buttered white.

The hopes it contains like children

and if the earth is inherited

not by the nested matryoshka doll,
dark-eyed, red-cheeked
whale-white big-bellied
with the children and grandchildren
she carries under the great stretched
coverlet of her skin

but by the virgin doll,
unbound, uninvested in futures,
who rubs herself *there*, a genie
warming the world for a moment
before she vanishes

will the skin-bag hold?
still be strong enough
to carry a future or two
arriving from a distance,
with or without star,
after a long march
down, through, out across the fields,
expelled, exiled, expired, exhumed?

Landscape with woman and flashlight

Her fellow homeless, teeming bodies
huddled with lice, odors of garbage
and worse, have already scattered
ahead of the oncoming storm.
She lifts her flashlight,

plays the beam across nearby doors.
Behind one door, noise as of
a pump handle being worked.
Her immigrant childhood flashes

before her: foreign eyes downcast,
fathers washing at the pump,
mothers' lips moving in silent
dirge for disasters left behind,

disasters to come. No wide new world
anywhere, just exile of myth, space
that frames bridges. She imagines
the people safe behind the door. Or

caught there. Remembers the baby
once trapped in her unlighted womb,
killed before it could escape
to cast its light, cut through
the darkness of the world.

My mother's fears, seen from an airplane

Not those volcanic needle peaks casting knife-
blade shadows that slice down into the earth
and vanish.
No.
Those khaki hills standing in pools of darkness
that spread slowly across the plain
where we both live.

Now at this station

A person has been sent from headquarters to help us find
trains that do not jerk like bucks gone mad at the upstate
county fair where there are no trains or buses and people
drive fast and hard and road kill ends up on dinner plates.
There, in winter, often there is not food enough even for
the children, and parents must decide each day which child
will go without eating. Road kill is tasty and tender if prop-
erly cooked. The body aches for more. Hunters are warned
to stay clear of the woods when the police are searching for
people hungry in lonely cabins. Human or animal, flesh
is to flesh as dust is to dust, even if animals do not ride in
trains or cars. The person from headquarters can help us
find out which track is right for us. For other questions
there is no help.

Advice on preparing for a role not often performed here anymore

Shrouding yourself
in the winding white summer curtains
and standing
downcast-eyed and window-framed
while your playmates sing
"Here Comes the Bride"

is easier done

when you have watched your mother's back
arch over the washtubs under the cellar window,
when you have helped her
haul the basket of wet curtains up the stairs
and hang them on the nail-studded wooden stretcher frame
leaned against the back wall of the house,
when you have left pearls of fingertip blood
around the nailholes in the edges of the curtains.

Electra in the kindergarten bathroom

In that slag-heap
of peach plastic babydoll bodies flung
into the toy bassinet near the bathroom door,
there must be three who look like us,

my sister strangled by her cord,
my sister killed by a hole in her heart,
and me,

three blood-covered turds pushed out
in duty to a husband. Surely my mother's body
wrapped the cord around the neck,
drilled the hole in the heart,
pushed to kill, with a whirring
and a blueing and a convulsing
of our lips and limbs. Surely she knew,
from the way I kicked the walls of her womb,
that I would not be a friend to her.

And Electra?

How was it for her?

I can tell you

I can tell you that from her father she learned
to speak with few words
fix faucets
watch the sky
feel the warning signals of her mother's storms

I can tell you how she felt
skipping down the street
to kiss her father coming home from work:
happy to be on the right side

I can tell you how it was for her when
her father said he would be there
the day they found the cure
cried because he could no longer
push the lawn mower
hard small oblong pellets rolled down
inside his trouser legs to the ground
his face became the face
of a man who is saying goodbye
and cannot find the door

Electra hissed at by a swan

As if she sensed I was coming
from the room of my dying father

As if she smelled death in my clothes,
saw it in my walk

As if she knew I was
husbandless, childless,
dry, cold, sunk in myself,
dust-bag, bone-bag,
mother-hater,
not to be trusted near her young

As she thought me befouled

As if my grief at father's dying
were not enough to redeem me

Situation with window

I did what I could for him.
Wiped the runnels of sweat
out of the pockets in his cheeks.
Folded the paper and fanned him.
Pushed his bed to the window
so that he could get some air.

I asked them to move me
to another hospital, he said.
I told them I don't belong
in this neighborhood, he said.
I asked them see
my situation as it is, he said.

Color scheme

On this Icelandic hillside,
purplish-red the seed-heads
of thickset rhubarb stalks standing
firm in their leaf-clump nests
against the ocean gale.

Oceans of time ago,
white my New York Irish
father's belly-skin, pulled-up
hospital gown, surgery scar,
stalk that made me
lying placid in its nest.

Grey-white the cliffs of Ireland.
What color the longboats
that ferried monks and slaves and settlers
from Ireland to Iceland to Ireland?

Many-colored the sheep and lambs
that graze these rock-hilled
sea-swallowed islands where poverty
turned lives to stone, drove the emigrant
ships against the wind.

Green the roots that bind
across oceans. Across the veil.

Truth in teaching

1.

The atrium was the place in the Latin book where the nun shrieked at us for our grammar mistakes. She was short and square, with blue eyes that watered and a face that reddened. Nothing else of her could be divined under her black headdress and habit. Off the page were the inner rooms where the Roman family ate and slept. The straight-backed *mater familias* was dressed in a peplum that fell in pleats to the floor. In the light-filled atrium my thoughts flitted amid the clashes that echoed in English and Latin: Caesar with the Gauls, Christians with lions, the nun with the call to serve Christ, my mother with her voices, vibrating through our wooden-box house.

2.

What to teach soldiers: That they are always to catalogue hard beds, cold floors, drafty mess halls, bread, and beans. That their struggle is between style and the need for nerves that do not skitter at the blush of a gun. That foxglove is known to stand up to every breeze. That the ancestors, patriotic, always saluted it.

Portrait of a come-back kid

Done and gone.
Yet he did pick up his bed and walk,
whistling past the rabble-rousing
crowd of rubber-neckers hugging the wall.
(Not a bed, really more a cheap
lime-green plastic litter stained
with who knows what and how.)
And he does have that

new job. Puts on
a waiter's white jacket and black bow-tie,
yells to customers waving their hands,
Yes, sir, I try to fly, maybe I'll succeed.
He can't be in two places at once, yet
he pretends he's a functioning bird,
refuses to show for the second going.

This poem is about a man

banging on a party wall, demanding
peace and quiet, dammit,
in this city of streets
flooded with sound

when maybe what he wants is the gleam
of a woman's rings
or
a kinked-dick charm
to glow on the rim of his dreams,
unlock his cold neck chain,
let in sweet chariots

that could swing him high and low,
sing holy-oiled lullabies.
drown out the clash
of the engines of death.

Saturday night at the saloon

The special *du jour* is dainty:
three-minutes stones
coddled by the Cook, dropped
into boiling salted water,
while the parrot rails and rants
about nutritional needs. There's
a brawl going on at the bar:

American heroes,
fresh from poking at cows,
enforce their claims recorded
in *The Book of People Who Did It
Their Way.* The watching parrot
quiets, tilts her head,
rests her cheek on her wing. Outside,

the horses read the weather-sky,
nuzzle the hitching rail,
prepare for the rumps and feet
of the men who will light out
for the beginning of the world,
never find themselves.

In country, this night,

this sail through the desert, along
the road that sprouts blue grass,

the valley, the low-slung hills
where lambs tangle
in mint-leaf laces,

the springing forest of stumps,
the fields spattered with purple flowers,

the town besotted with sleep,

the scent of palm-trees
draped in garlands
of carved wooden beads,

the pebbled streets, the port,
the sunken ships,
no fixed sailing times

Townscape

Same soggy trees, geography
hard to hold eyes on, philosophy
of gone-without.

Library down to basics:
Britannica, an exhibit on Angels,
their names, attributes, orders, ranks,
pictures of them strumming their lutes,
their bare bunioned feet showing
beneath the hems of their windblown gowns.

Wind crests over the street. A move
that will mean death from quaking cold
if the town's not careful.

Somebody opens the trunk
of a two-door Rose. Odor of earth
and dark wet leaves. Brilliant
salmon-pink bursts of mushrooms
fitful as matinee idols. Dust in
every whorl and groove.

Still no train, just the two local buses.

Landscape with music

How great the corners,
the disheveled blocks,
the shadow markets,
the sweet spots up on the roofs.

The hum sets the tone.
Up and about in the high-times park,
a goth-blues group sizzles
in the heat, sings

the sorrows of the city ghosts,
the cries of this People of the Will
bounded by their bright towers,
their sun-quenched view.

Even time is torched.
The birds don't swim.
Whispers rain through the air.
This city is its summer,

a one-trick vandal that comes in
mad.

Uncanny

The way the same things show up over and over for counting. Always deeply practical. Always impeccably polite.

On summer nights, we gather in the square to hear numbers beamed out and objects called up for the count.

Dry quiet things are the most popular because they are easier to count up or down than are moist moving things.

There is no summer night without its count of the cars roaming in the commuter parking lot, the shadows of ships quietly moving offshore.

Counting brings to life our groves of still white trees, our acorns in the park, our sparrows nibbling on droppings under the outdoor restaurant tables. Everything is so open out here. In fact, calls for head counts go out over the public address system. Sooner or later enough heads that the counting of crosses can begin.

I go to the village every day,

buy milk and bread and paper,
say hello and goodbye, act *as if.*
When the trains come in, I look
through the open doors
of the mail cars, watch
the old men in plaid flannel shirts
sort foreign letters, flat and pale
as headstones. So many years
away from home, I still remember

the small white stones that filled
with the heat of summers
until they burst
and lay broken in the fields.
Coming upon them as we worked,
we would keep them for good-luck charms,
fallen stars now part of our land,
which had congealed in a crust around them,
until, suddenly remembering what they were,

they had exploded out of their graves
and been restored to light. The sky here
is a washed-stone grey, discreet,
respectful of unscheduled change.
If I went home, after all these years
of *as if* in this country of *Them,*
could I still think in a language
that people would know?

There's confusion in the land, but

here's an answer:
This momma-house (no dogs permitted)
is storm-tossed cloths hung on dry
lines between poles. What's the question?
When will you leave it? Not this spring,

with your boils already blooming.
This past winter,
the authorities leveled a 300-year-old
dune left out of their promise of land.
A critical crack: shifting ground

makes for a bumpy ride, the kind of test
nothing in school can teach you. So far
at least you kids are still okay: little
hillocks of joy in a beach-grass act,
playing it safe on the lit-up sand.

Remember your test number. Because
sooner or later it's Sayonara, all you kids
in your sunsuits. Whatever your grade,
you too get to hide in the ground.

The speech of birds

Winter streets fill with the voices of shipwrecked sailors who have been windblown to shore and lured to movie houses where they hang their dogtags on pegs when they arrive.

Moving pictures fill blackness with long murmurs and sudden romantic or dramatic clicks that bob and connect at the end.

The sailors' dreams are short and soft. Whether we have already heard or almost heard or never heard them before, we keep count and record them in the town ledger.

We treat dreams as we treat any other cold-water creature: Put out a salt lick to keep them coming—mostly clawed, barb-tailed, winged worm-serpents. The theory is that if we plant serpents' teeth in our gardens an army of serpents will spring up to defend us, if we drink their blood we shall never die, if we cut off their heads we shall understand the speech of birds.

Spin this:

The latest bird-thunder launch.
Clips, claws, wing parts,
bundles of feathers screaming
over our town. Flight of our feet
down to the streets

where steel beasts germinate
from wave forms of thunder
and a bird-chirp recording.
Are we fooled
when they cheep like the birds?

How many streets
to the end of the world?
How many beasts
between us and our bread?
Where's the streaming stairway

to our many-stars general,
god of our seed, bark of our birds?
Can we put our mark on him?
Will he reject us? No matter

any of this. The beast of our bellies
continues its spinward march.
Nice program. It's ours.

Just off the hummingbird highway

down a winding packed-sand road
    with serious crickets
        nattering in the grassy shoulders,

our right little tight little
    city lies in the path of everywhere else.
    In half a thousand years

no one has ever mapped all
    its comings and goings. It has

old pastel spirit, patient sea, restless new
walls made of blue glass blocks,
    view-yards where we watch

the deep past
    dance, dive, rise to the angel
        in the rafters of the squinting sky.

At night it sleeps
    in the shadows cast
        by the grass and the sea, the five stars hung

from hooks in the wilderness sky,
    the moon soft and sandy in the west.
        The river babbles about the gibbons
            roosting in the trees.

About eating

I'm off my feed this week,
like an animal sick or wounded.
Or maybe our food has gone sour.
Especially meat of all kinds.
I've eaten venison, goat, rabbit, bull
fresh from the matador's strike.
Never dog or cat, although
they feed off *us* without a qualm.
Our skittish grey cat was fed
the leavings off our table.
Not built to breed,
every litter she dropped was sickly,

soon stopped suckling, died.
My farm-bred father
explained about animals like her:
The farmers gave them a few chances,
then slaughtered them for food.
Early orphaned, he wanted
a family. My mother produced.
The first died stillborn, the second
died of a hole in her heart.
In our long family feast,
I fed on my mother, she on my father,
the two of them fed on me.

Crossing

It is seven A.M. and raining
when I awaken in my berth
in Kansas City, Missouri.
The Midwest. Truman Country.
The station is big enough and stone enough
for any president. Outside,
men in yellow windbreakers stand,
hands in pockets, shuffling feet,
not looking up to the window
where they would see me
lying in state in pink pajamas.

Last night I crossed their country.
In the dining car a man talked
about riding in coach, not sleeper.
"So as not to be alone," he said.
"After fifty years of marriage,
being alone is hell."
The word has long been out:
Hell is other people.

It is not my country,
that hot and bitter fault
where life-plates grind at odds.
I always ride in sleeper.
Lie back in solitary state
and try to measure on the map
how far I have come and gone,
how much farther I must travel.
I have not come all this country alone
for nothing.

II.

The early life of the righteous

We have my uncle the used-truck dealer
to thank for it. The one who looked out
at his lot after a snowstorm
and saw the truth and the way.
Who taught us to shovel,
heft barrels of snow into the trucks,
drive through the late-day streets
to the river, haul and tug and dump

into the black water, where the snow
swirled like spoiled milk
reaching for a sink drain
and slid down into darkness.
Sleepless and sour, our lives churned.
We trashed cycle after cycle of seasons.

Learned to start over and over.

I went on living

because the child said it was pouring,
and I believed her. It was the least
I could do to say "Thank you"

for the paws of the dog all muddy
from its walk along the shoulder
of the road,

for her red umbrella at her back,
for her gaze all blurred
by the rain as it settled into tears

on her face, so like my own
half-hidden inside my hood
and shining with mist and pain

and the purity I felt
at the thought that I should never
need this reunion again.

Storm-gazer. Sometimes thought

he *was* the storm. Sitting at the window,
he watched his house ripple
on the blue glass face of the office tower
across the street. In this country, filled

with views, a sky that was naked
clouded his eyes, undid his mind.
He had odd battles with thoughts.
The room in his head echoed
to the sounds of their dueling,
their gymnastics crammed
into too small a space and time.

He carved stones with the names
of the forgotten and gone.
Always right, insulting to his betters,
he found darkness easier to bear
than light. Something to do with seeing
the depth and shade of sadness.

Then the dinner party, the long night,
the two lost days. That third day,
morning, early. The handsome
young man—his lover, maybe?—
sunning himself on a rock,
who told the visiting women,
"He's not here, he up and left."

Landscape with birds

Consider these matters of chance:
Birds eat twice their weight
in stone-cold food.
Birds have shat on my hair.
Consider the past of the robin
I once cupped in my hands:
I felt the fear in its pounding heart
and darting eye, let it go
streaking off to a tree.

Consider the besotted bird that crashed
into a mirror in an orphanage hall.
Vanity of vanities, the wages of sin.
The nuns shoveled its body into a bag.
Consider the gutted birds
that lorded it over the orphanage parlor
from the glass-front curio cabinet.
Consider my mother, fruit
of the orphanage womb,

who channeled her fear into a beak,
tore at the walls and the ceiling.
Consider her cries, smothered
by mop and pail, or passing
through a telephone line
under a row of judgment birds,
passing from bird to listening bird,
circling back to the burial cairn.

So many messages, so little space.

Water babies

Bruised and blue the broken
cuttlefish that struggled past
the weirkeeper's lodge to write
their stories on the sandbar.
I wrung them out, hung them up,
deflated, dripping ink.

Rough the peeling painted
doors of the hospital room,
smooth the streaming velvet tide
in which I held my mother's thin
cool hands, fish drifting,
dry as death.

Metamorphosis

                                    Yesterday,
as if recently dead, I saw myself
passionate fruit, swinging
from the persimmon tree in my yard.

Then cut down, crumpled on the ground,
oxen tonguing me, head to foot,
until my body turned

round-eyed fish, breathless, marooned,
cooked, eaten, made flesh.
Slappering on the sand, I pray
for an incoming wave to carry me home.

                                    Tomorrow,
I may be raving to the fishermen. Or
food for *their* fish. Operations
best performed in the morning,
when I have the whole day's dying before me.

As the crow flies

As it now flies,
in a warplaned sky,
black pendant snagged
on a chain of clouds.

Small victories.

The crow breathes in
our lost kings,
breathes them back out as gods.

Addition by subtraction.

Eruption

There's been a shaking in the belly. Eleven eruptors faded and dead. The next one is going to be a stretch-our-world. There's a long season ahead, and it's hard to ignore these early signs. Put them all together and we've got us rolling on a start. We're the play, we're the stage, with lighting of stones and throwing of torches to burn the bloom off the edge of our days, we're the theatre for the hits that will come, most of them not our call.

That was no contest, Angel.

I was dough in your hands,
overrisen, in need of the work
you came to do:
punch me down, knead me,
reduce me to fit within
the limits set for my world.
Then you moved on

to your next task. Left me to wonder
if you envy us our buttery flesh,
regret your unbodied self, your lack
of a form you can call your own,
your need to borrow a shape
every time you visit our world. If
you and I would be happy

transmuted for good, as dough
is changed unalterably into bread.
What if change is the name of our nature,
is what we are? Then our world
is a moving boundary. After the body
becomes ash, we rise again.

It is best for hares

to stay covered in winter. Even a bare
November sky can bear witness
to the places where they hide.
It is important to keep a hare
covered by the hunters' guns.
The best hare is a hare startled on a run.
The most important hare is a hare
once bitten by a dog. A biting
dog cannot bark, but there are other
uses for barking dogs, provided
there is a translator
to record barks and yaps and growls,
tell the hunters what hare news the dog
is barking, create a bark history
that can be analyzed
to determine how shy hares
can be run to earth.

Pastorale

Stick-legged shadows
of springing does
come to rest under a tree.
A hen announces presentation
of the fruit of her loins.
Love like hers turns any
morning into speckles of light.
The lake hums. Overhead,
bluebottle flies, dragonflies,
the odd robin or two. Pursed
lips of a fish punch a hole
in the surface of the water.
It's so morning, this lake,
that rowboat, that woman
leaning over the gunwale, face
roiling the truth of reflection.

Millennium

The ice will be wiped clean with a stroke of the pen. The past will be broken in a striking way. But even in this extraordinary time, encourage your children to understand and respect the importance of tradition and precedent. Let them stand on the letter of the law so that they will be tall enough to look out through the widow at the Promised Land. Open the window so that they can throw out one of their dolls and watch her fly through the air and land sprawled on the stoop, her legs spread wide, her torso twisted, her head turned up to look at the house, at the window, and at your children looking down at her and arguing the fine points of the ancient and honorable art of defenestration.

First manned flight

Fingertips wingspanned,
I recited my instructions.

Looked down at a tower,
wondered, *Are those really
people in there?*

Flew closer, saw: *Yes,
really, how normal.*

Identified oncoming object:
angel poised
to celebrate the lightness
of things that fall.

Perfect time to fly
into the sunset.
Just to the edge.
Then one inch more.

On throwing away a piece of dental floss in the yard for use by a nest-building bird

but what if
the bird tugs
on a sticking-out
end of the floss

and tugs and tugs and
the nest falls apart
before the babies are grown

can they be healed
after home has been
cracked wide open?

What I want to know, Death,

is, when I decide
to say Enough, say
Gun, Pill, Plunge,

snatch my life from
your spindle, cut it
to the length *I* want,

will you be happy
that *I* came for *you?*

Then the worm turns

Let me start there,
with this sign of a new order, a change
in the general tide: The galleys
rowed by teams of worms harnessed
to squirm in tandem. They love garbage:
melon rind, banana peel, eggshells,
coffee grounds, old lettuce. Everything
that lives under our river-park outhouse
with the blue wooden door. A pound of worms

eat a half-pound of garbage in a day.
Churn, aerate, digest in darkness,
turn waste into gold, or at least new
earthstuff. Dropped on shredded newsprint,
they burrow away from the light.
How many pounds to eat a news story,
an editorial, an ad for perfumed bras?
To recycle the shells and casings and bodies
that litter our post-world ground? Once

I smashed a worm. I still shudder
when police cars shriek past my house,
their echo-systems crashing
against the branches of the willows in the park.
In Old English, *wyrm* was worm, serpent, dragon.
What does it mean, that a single word
once did all the earthcrawling work of the world?
What does it mean, my concern with these rulers

of death, decay, transformation, return?
One day, sunning themselves
like sweet warm strings of words,
they will have a party on my dock.
It will not be my party, yet
I will be guest and host.

Landscape with trial

Reports of iron crosses falling out of the sky
are greatly exaggerated. Still: three people
struck while walking in the park,
no small toll in our country, where unlovely
words and deeds, the stuff of confession,
swing from the coils of copper wire
that we wear like fetters on our wrists.

Yesterday, down by the salmon weir bridge,
we watched the open-air court try
a fisherman taken *in flagrante*. He pleaded
decanting of the stream into a cut-glass
holy-water bottle. He pleaded reinvention
of the salmon and its leap for those it loves,
its solemn voyage upstream against the wombwash.

He pleaded our ancientness, our memory,
our mothers and sons and our holy spirit
broken on the wheel, the better to serve.
The court found him guilty of treason.
In our country there is never a shortage
of servitude. Ordered away from the bridge,
we took what was offered us and left.

Footnote to a history of the Flood

The doors and windows were gone,
the house stood open
to every weather.
The men tramped in and out
to use the toilet. Decent men,
but after the first day
we women and the children went
in the back yard, behind a tangle of debris,
bones, and torn-out hair.

In the front yard,
bees dried themselves
around the burning bodies.
God promised:
Never again water, but fire.
We stuffed the hair
into ticking for mattresses
to fill the city shelters.
For later, when the lights
go out for good.

III.

Situation at the river

Yesterday I saw birds on branches.
This is March and the hatters are stricken.
Probably a toxin in the last
of the potatoes in the winter barrel.
Schizophrenia is endemic in these
potato lands. It's over-cold to search
for frenzied bottom-runners lounging
on the river bed. A lizard
may be no less a reptile
when made into shoes and a belt
to hold my summer dress close
to my body. It's too soon to know

what's bedded under the glass
blanket breaking up on the river.
The rising water's black, no matter
a white body was found in it once.
The lines of March-mad
marathoners toning on the road
flow past. Their bodies are gaunt. Mine's
a noisome watch, its ticking
just slightly off the wing-beat
of the watching robin. Tocksplash.
Mind the bed as it swims to me.

An easy way to explain hiding

The way the knife blade plunges
to the hilt, buries itself, hungry,
in the loaf of bread,
the block of butter.
The way the bread, the butter,
lean in to warm the blade,
enjoy its edge pressing
into their quiet flesh.

The way the handle pursues
its secret dream
to be the tool
that tears out the blade.
The way the blade quivers
with loss, rights itself,
unknowing

of the hunger in the wound.

The suffering of separation

Always a clock
watching from a tower.
Always a woman who rises early,
scuttles through the cold streets
to the all-night store.
A long-termed man who leaves her
to hose down the city sidewalks.

Always a sleeper getting up from a grate.
A bread-line forming on the temple steps
where coins change hands. A wailing
wall with posters of the missing.
An off-course calf bawling
for its lost mother.

To every calf its cow,
to every clock its tower.
The suffering of separation
never becomes us.
It remains itself, a smudge
in the sky above the parking lot,
the mall, the birds taking stock.

Incandescence

Just as you ring the doorbell,
I finish reading Barth's account of what happened
when pirates flowed across the whoreship *Cyprian*
and took their booty in every part of the ship,
including the rigging, where one of the women clung
until her pursuer came up and upon and into her from behind,
while a crew member watching from the deck below
clapped his hands and laughed

just as you ring the doorbell

your coat already unbuttoned

already thrown on a chair
already joined by your trousers and briefs

your legs already bearing us to the bed, where
I smooth the fine straight reddish hairs that lie
in quiet rows across your belly
and remember other pirates I have read about

such as

victorious armies settling accounts.
In landlocked cities where there were no riggings,
they pursued their booty to the tops of towers.
In riverside cities, they nailed the women
naked and alive to doors and sent them floating
down to the sea. Flowed around and through
the ruins, calling "Woman! Woman!" Here the ships
were the churches, where the bells rang wildly
all night long. By morning, when the men of the cities
came with wheelbarrows to cart their women away,
the thick soft ropes of the bells were swaying slowly.

From these scenes I turn away
turn back turn away
wantingnotwanting to watch.
Turn away and stroke you there
and think about

my unit of female partisans, pouring out from the forest,
falling upon you hurling you down spread-eagling you
pegging you to the ground
while I
fumbling in your trousers
draw it out into the chilly air.
Perhaps I enter it with the long nicked blade
of my knife. Then we melt back into the forest,
leaving you to water this one small piece of earth
with your blood. Or perhaps we take turns
lowering ourselves upon you, cursing
when you do not rise to meet us. Until,
tiring of you, I order you taken
to the woods and shot.

The fear, under deep cover

I have gone to business school and law school. I have been living here with my friends for three years but I guess I will never lose that look off my face. Living here is very warm. I wouldn't call it stereotypical but it has a lot of bland reality. The patio is the neutral space where we talk. We try to keep things clean but never really succeed. The sofa has cockroach nests. The cigarette butts pile up. We are preparing for a party that will be a friends kind of thing. We have been hanging in here all day trying to be characters. We are putting in an effort to have a good time, or a mellow time at least. I feel my social skills are not adequate. The camera makes me shy. I don't want my image stolen. I look as if I am trying to get where I am even if I am sitting on the sofa on the patio. I could put a burlap bag over my head, then I wouldn't see. This is a crazy block. It's like drawing down a dream. We have access and go to all the best places. When there is no party, there is talk of one. My life is great but it's not all that. It knows no loyalty. It doesn't care who I am. It doesn't care how much I love the people who depend on me. Doing it or not is not up to me. If there is going to be evidence later of what transpired, I had better be on my best behavior.

Innocence of the onion

When my ghost cries from hunger,
I feed her onions. Peel off their crackling,
papery coats, unpack layer after layer,
outer to inner, of pungent flesh.
Napkin tucked under chin,
knife and fork upraised in fisted hands,
she shrieks for more. Peel faster.
Shovel onion into her mouth.
She howls for more. Peel, peel,

outside to inside to heart. She screams
for more, more, faster, faster. Not
enough. Nowhere enough. Never
enough. Onion juice runs
down my fingers. I poke them
into her eyes. Let her feel
the price I pay
for this ancient, infinite famine.

In a related late-news development,

police report that around noon a seven-foot clown
scaled the fifty-story water tower down
by the waterfront. He says he is buying a farm
and wants to get the full flavor of its charm
from above. When asked his name,
he says it's Napoleon as in the French emperor.
Expresses delight that the cops can climb to that height.
Further discussion has turned to argument.
Maintenance crews have lent the police
nuisance removal gear. One by one
cops are moving onto the ledge. A lone
robin is keeping the clown company. Heaven
for a bird is a tree and a waving bough,
but the robin is staying the course, even
flew at a cop who got too close. Now
the Mayor has announced that the sky
is off limits to climbers. The news camera eye
is picking up a stranger on the shore,
a sign asking the clown to wave.

Astrolabe

Someone will try to persuade you of the narrowness of your outlook. This will amaze you, though you may think that the minor angles have little meaning. Triangle, rectangle, quadrangle: Line them up in order of size, the way the nuns at school lined you all up in the beginning, you first, as the smallest. Quadrangle, rectangle, triangle: Line them up in alphabetical order, the way the nuns lined you up at the end, you with your medium-range H-name lost in a cloud. In either case, the width of the angle that you make with the earth and the sun will astonish you. The question is, How many angels can dance in an angle?

Working with Splash

The falls are on the edge of town, very close to the lab where I work on the project for the installation of mirrors, mist, and artificial sun-lights along the riverfront.

In the lab, righteousness is about correct branding. If I discover a belief and don't label it correctly, I can't install it. Just because a belief was discovered in a lab doesn't mean the lights last forever and the mirrors don't need to be cleaned.

Usually the skyline is solid and full. But during the summer months, the water roils and the rain clouds tumble into the global positioning system. These are the months when we punch a hole in the lab ceiling and climb up to check the world outside.

Cemetery, summer afternoon

Whiff of skunk cabbage
from the marigold beds.
White slime slug tracks
woven into the grass.

This is no country
for plastic wreaths.

Along the horizon,
bridges of lightning bolted
to the charcoal sky.
Between two tombs, a man jerks off.

Enigma

Hear the body's
large-bore thoughts rattle
the walls of its box

the mind
clack heel to toe
through streets of blooming bodies

She knew the game to play with him,

her bird-god with beaky nose,
receding chin, neckless round
body large above his skinny legs.
In no time she was streaming in satin,
braving the tornado in his eyes.
All he wanted was chaos
brought out of order. She
wanted the secret and rule
of his body. He went political,
made a full-scale statement
on the values of carnage. She
went flat-out for neatness.
Lightning slivered and strafed,
flashed their hunger.

Our stories now in progress

These just in:

> Shortage of the glue
> that holds the sky firm
> against the clouds.
> Woman tired of dying
> shoots funeral director.

In the beginning is the ending.

Beached whale

This is not Nantucket of the whaling days, when whole villages turned out to wonder at such sights. But we New Yorkers are not unfamiliar with the crashing of bodies on our shores. This one is pearl-gray, stained with darker patches of sweat and dirt, eyes closed, shopping bags piled around his head, mouth spouting snores and saliva. His shirt buttons and the rope belt holding his trousers have opened away from his blue-white blubber, which is swelling and ebbing like a running sea, while incoming tides of office workers foam around him on the concrete beach.

Sea Chantey

We too potted lobster, hauled
mackerel and herring, sailed until
Death scraped us clean of the barnacles
that dragged on our souls. Don't ask

how long it has taken the fish
to eat our bones clean,
how we give thanks
for the waves that massage us,
the fleet of your prayers
that sails above our heads.
We find it enough

to have become your culture:
Lodged in your memory,
we shape you, layer on layer, until
you become pearls,
like us unseen
by idle walkers on the beach.

Deep-time run

The horses run past the winepress,
halt covered with sins.
The last page of our calendar
turns a corner, crumbles into dust.

Forewarned, we refugee
to the church in the square.
Hunker down in the front-row pews,
watch the palm fronds wilt.

The tower bell chimes the year.
Cockleshells clack in the breeze,
drive the widows wild.

Before the altar, the working
wealthy slated for retraining
rant like the mad hatters
of headgear times.

Our skin turns grainy, looks
like cauliflower gone to brown.

After brain surgery

Flash of the scalpel as it grazes
the damp loamy surface of his brain,
excises the orange mushrooms
that purse fluted lips into the glare.

Afterwards, he can still remember
a few rheumy details of his life:
thefts of honey, mostly, and his loss
of the picture of God he won at a raffle.

His words vaporize before
he finishes saying them. It is dark
inside the hard-shell black-box mind
where he made merry for so many years.

Pill

Do you feel
short, dark, doughy, little and low?

Experience fatigue, weak memory,
no interest in usual activities,

sad, blue, depressed,
enthusiasm put out at curb,

your heart racing to gilded cage?

If you've answered yes,
do you brake for cheap eats,

have you thought of yourself
as bitter pill?

The last hour of Lot's wife

Deer came down the slope:
one, two together, then others,
their heads up, eyes and nostrils
probing before they laid tongue
to her. There was no part of her

they did not pleasure. They even
entered her, licked her walls,
inside and out, till her womb bled
salt water, and she dissolved
into wonder at the memory.

This is how her body

endured: As long slow carve of ivory
Mother-and-Child. As fresco.
As Virgin among virgins in paintings
of walled gardens where she sat,
afternoons, with the other long-robed
golden-limbed girls. Embroidered.
Sang. Paged through hymnals.
Watched the others depart to be
handmaidens of lords, surety
for lands and castles and alliances,
containers and bearers of heirs.

How did such narrow bodies hold
a kicking foetus? Such tiny breasts
give suck? What was the pain
of menstruation and morning sickness,
the terror of childbirth,
in castles without light, heat, air,
running water, their rooms open
and defenseless? In later years,
did those girls-become-women dream
of achieving what she achieved,

Virgin Birth? Or at least
of closing their bodies to their husbands
after the birth of the thirteenth heir?
Did she herself dare to dream
her body whole again, entire, unbreached?
Not gate of heaven, not house of gold,
not star of the sea. Not idol.
Not work of art. Just body.
Just self. For herself.

The first clue I had

was when my piss turned
that funny color like
when I pour boiling water
over a teabag and before
the water has got real dark.
It was just sometimes at first
but soon it was every time
and dark right fresh out
like the teabag had been
sitting in it for awhile. Then

red things started passing,
bits of red peppers fried too long
till they got dark and shrunk up.
Next came shreds of stuff
like meat all grey and wrinkled
from standing in water.
What my body is doing I think
is it's making more body
and pieces of it are breaking off.
And fresh meat bleeds
when it's cut.

Doing bone time

is what comes of that toss of the dice
that ends with the 206 bones of the body
inventing stories to be told into the air,
straining to remember
the trees in the childhood back yard.
A bone is a report that an *I* was here,
scrabbled hard through its time,
ended in the ground,
good yard food for the dogs.
Bone time is the flow of us. Our feet rumble,
our fists chant, our bellies shake

in time with what's going on *now, here*
on the shifting earthplates honeycombed
with the cells where we live and work
above the billions of our ancestors
dispersed into the tissues of the land.
No matter our throw of the dice,
the ground quakes when it must,
the honeycomb cracks,
essence of forebear escapes upward
into the everyday smoke of our campfires,
the bones of our hard handsome race.

Acknowledgments

"About Eating," *Lilies and Cannonballs Review*, Vol. 2, #1, Spring/Summer 2005, p. 25.

"Advice on preparing for a role not often performed here any more," *The Next Parish Over: A Collection of Irish-American Writing*, Patricia Monaghan, ed. Minneapolis MN: New Rivers Press, 1993, p. 165.

"An easy way to explain hiding," *Eclipse*, Vol. Thirteen, Fall 2002, p. 140.

"And Electra?" *The Quarterly* [defunct] , #5, Spring 1988, p. 196.

"As the crow flies," *The 7th Annual Brevitas Festival of the Short Poem* (anthology), 2010, p. 29.

"Astrolabe" [prose poem], *The Prose Poem* [defunct], #1, 1991 [unpaginated].

"Beached Whale" [prose poem], *The Quarterly* [defunct], #8, Winter 1988, p. 168.

"Cemetery, Summer Afternoon," *Fulcrum: An annual of poetry and aesthetics*, Fulcrum 6, Summer 2007, p. 165.

"Crossing," *The Paris Review*, #132, Fall 1994, p. 22.

"Doing bone time," *Nimrod International Journal*, Vol. 3, #2, Spring/Summer 2000, p. 145.

"The early life of the righteous," *Dominion Review*, Vol. XV – 1997, p. 116.

"Eight Things A Day, That's All," *The Literary Review*, Vol. 43, #4, Summer 2000, p. 549, under title "Declaring the Wild."

"Electra hissed at by a swan," *The Paris Review*, #132, Fall 1994, p. 25.

"Electra in the kindergarten bathroom," *The Next Parish Over: A Collection of Irish-American Writing.*
Patricia Monaghan, ed. Minneapolis MN: New Rivers Press, 1993, p. 164.

"Enigma," *The 7th Annual Brevitas Festival of the Short Poem* (anthology), 2010, p. 29.

"The fear, under deep cover" appeared in both *Oregon East,* Volume XXXI, 2000, p. 57, and *Northwest Review*, Volume 38, No. 3, 2000.

"The first clue I had," *The New York Quarterly*, #32, Spring 1987, p. 87.

"First Manned Flight," *Fulcrum: An annual of poetry and aesthetics,* Fulcrum 6, Summer 2007, p. 166.

"Footnote to a history of the flood," *Western Humanities Review*, Vol. XLVII #4, Winter 1993, p. 372.

"The hopes it contains like children," *Confluence*, Fall 1999, p. 20; The Minnesota Review, #50-51, Fall 1999, p. 30.

"I go to the village every day," *Southern Humanities Review*, Vol. 38 #3, Summer 2004, p. 271.

"Incandescence," *The Quarterly* [defunct], #5, Spring 1988, pp. 197-198.

"Innocence of the Onion," *Southern Humanities Review*, Vol. 38 #3, Summer 2004, p. 270.

"It is best for hares," *Good Foot: A Poetry Magazine*, Spring 2005, #6, p. 63.

"I went on living," *Dominion Review*, Vol. XV – 1997, p. 119.

"Landscape with birds," *Westview*, Vol. 17 #2, Spring/Summer 1998, p. 39.

"Landscape with freight train," *Connecticut River Review*, Vol. 16 #2, Summer/Fall 1996, p. 23.

"Landscape with trial," *The William and Mary Review*, Vol. 35 – 1997, p. 90.

"The last hour of Lot's wife," *Flyway*, Vol. 2 #2, Fall 1996, pp. 68-69.

"Metamorphosis," *Descant* 2002, Vol. 41, p. 63; *Willow Review*, Vol. XXX, Spring 2003, p. 34.

"Millennium" both *Margie – The American Journal of Poetry*, Vol. 3/2004, p. 154 and [Finalist in First Annual "Strong Rx Medicine" Poetry Contest, 2004; Russell Edson, judge].

"My mother's fears, seen from an airplane," *The Quarterly* [defunct], #5, Spring 1988, p. 195.

"Now at this station," *The Dirty Goat*, #18, January 2008, p. 168; *Quercus Review*, # 8 (2008), p. 67.

"Pastorale," *California Quarterly*, Vol. 32, #4, 2006, p. 16.

"Poem for Memorial Day," section "1," *The Pikeville Review*, Summer 1999, p. 10 (under title "United States Poem Number 4"); section "2," *decomP magazinE*, August 2011.

"Portrait of a come-back kid," *Kinesis* [defunct], Vol. 5 #9, Sept. 1996, p. 6.

"Saturday night at the Saloon," *The Laurel Review*, Vol. 38 #1, Winter 2004, p. 102.

"She Knew The Game to Play With Him," *Sanskrit Literary-Arts Magazine*, Vol. 36, 2005, p. 28.

"Situation at the river," *Many Mountains Moving*, Twelfth Issue (2001), Vol. IV, #3, p. 19.

"Situation with window," *Lullwater Review*, Fall 1999, Vol. X, #1, p. 39.

"Sometimes he thinks about walking," *Limestone* 2002, p. 70.

"Stormgazer. Sometimes thought," *Phantasmagoria*, Fall/Winter 2003, Vol. 3 #2, p. 89.

"That most American thing," *Fulcrum: An annual of poetry and aesthetics*, Fulcrum 6, [2007]2008, p. 165.

"That was no Contest, Angel," *RiverSedge*, Vol. 18, # 1, Spring 2005, p. 33.

"Then the worm turns," *The Spoon River Poetry Review*, Vol. XXVI, # 1, Winter/Spring 2001, p. 80.

"This is how her body," *The Best of Writers at Work 1995*, ed. W. Scott Olsen, San Antonio TX: Pecan Grove Press, p. 95.

"This is a poem about a man," *South Dakota Review*, Vol. 40, # 3, Celebrating New York City, Fall 2002, p. 111; *WestWind Review. Poetry and Fiction Anthology*, 22nd Anthology, 2003, p. 11 [under title "This poem is about a man"].

"Those Of Us Who Remember," *RiverSedge*, accepted for future publication.

"Townscape," earlier version published in *Sojourner: The Women's Forum*, Vol. 22, # 3 (November 1996), page 33.

"United States Poem," *The Chariton Review*, Vol. 26, # 2, Fall 2000, p. 103 [under title"United States Poem Number 8"].

"Water babies," *Western Humanities Review*, Vol. XLVII #4, Winter 1993, p. 372.

"What I want to know, Death," *The Dirty Goat*, #18, January 2008, p. 169.

"Yet another bout of meaningful madness," *The Louisville Review*, Vol. 51, Spring 2002, p. 66.

About NYQ Books™

NYQ Books™ was established in 2009 as an imprint of The New York Quarterly Foundation, Inc. Its mission is to augment the *New York Quarterly* poetry magazine by providing an additional venue for poets already published in the magazine. A lifelong dream of NYQ's founding editor, William Packard, NYQ Books™ has been made possible by both growing foundation support and new technology that was not available during William Packard's lifetime. We are proud to present these books to you and hope that you will continue to support The New York Quarterly Foundation, Inc. and our poets and that you will enjoy these other titles from NYQ Books™:

Barbara Blatner	*The Still Position*
Amanda J. Bradley	*Hints and Allegations*
rd coleman	*beach tracks*
Joanna Crispi	*Soldier in the Grass*
Ira Joe Fisher	*Songs from an Earlier Century*
Sanford Fraser	*Tourist*
Tony Gloeggler	*The Last Lie*
Ted Jonathan	*Bones & Jokes*
Richard Kostelanetz	*Recircuits*
Iris Lee	*Urban Bird Life*
Linda Lerner	*Takes Guts and Years Sometimes*
Gordon Massman	*0.174*
Michael Montlack	*Cool Limbo*
Kevin Pilkington	*In the Eyes of a Dog*
Jim Reese	*ghost on 3rd*
F. D. Reeve	*The Puzzle Master and Other Poems*
Jackie Sheeler	*Earthquake Came to Harlem*
Jayne Lyn Stahl	*Riding with Destiny*
Shelley Stenhouse	*Impunity*
Tim Suermondt	*Just Beautiful*
Douglas Treem	*Everything so Seriously*
Oren Wagner	*Voluptuous Gloom*
Joe Weil	*The Plumber's Apprentice*
Pui Ying Wong	*Yellow Plum Season*
Fred Yannantuono	*A Boilermaker for the Lady*
Grace Zabriskie	*Poems*

Please visit our website for these and other titles:

www.nyqbooks.org